Begonias

A Wisley Handbook

Begonias

BILL WALL

Cassell

The Royal Horticultural Society

THE ROYAL HORTICULTURAL SOCIETY

Cassell Educational Limited
Villiers House, 41/47 Strand
London WC2N 5JE
for the Royal Horticultural Society

First published 1988
Second impression 1989
Second edition 1993

British Library Cataloguing in Publication Data
A catalogue record for this book is available from the British Library

ISBN 0–304–32069–2

Photographs by the Harry Smith Collection, Photos Horticultural and Bill Wall
Line drawings by Graham Wall

Phototypesetting by RGM Associates, Southport
Printed in Hong Kong by Wing King Tong Co. Ltd

Cover: *Begonia tuberosa* 'Pin Up' is one of the modern range of hybrids, with South American ancestors.
    Photograph by Photos Horticultural
Back cover: *Begonia serratipetala*, an attractive plant for a hanging basket.
p.1: Nonstop begonia 'Salmon Pink', a Multiflora tuberous hybrid.
    Photographs by the Harry Smith Collection
p.2: Rex begonias show a tremendous diversity of leaf shape and colour.

Contents

Introduction

Mention the word "begonia" to many people and they think of the tuberous begonias with their giant flamboyant flowers. Thousands of these are bought from garden centres and stores throughout the country in early spring, to be raised as pot plants for summer decoration in the home, while named varieties are lovingly tended by enthusiasts, for exhibition at flower shows in the late summer. Other people will associate the genus with the Semperflorens or Multiflora begonias, both of which are used for bedding out to give masses of colour in the garden from late spring to the first frosts.

However, in more recent years a number of foliage begonias have been appearing on the scene and have become popular as colourful evergreen houseplants, particularly the dwarf ones like 'Tiger Paws', 'Cleopatra' and B. mazae. These are showy throughout the year and are very easy to cultivate in the home in shady situations, where many other plants would not succeed. For their owners, inspired to look for further varieties, they open up a whole world of begonias – a group of plants which is probably more diverse in leaf colour and shape and more varied in form than any other, and often with the bonus of long-lasting flowers.

HISTORY

The genus is a very large one, containing over 2,000 species and several thousand hybrids. It includes many of our finest ornamental pot plants, noted for their magnificent flowers or for their remarkable, often iridescent, leaf colouring, as well as some most useful summer bedding plants for the garden. The genus was recognized as such in 1700 and named in honour of Michel Begon, a French botanist and administrator of Santo Domingo in the West Indies. However, a few plants had been discovered before this date which subsequently proved to be begonias. In 1649, the Mexican plant now known as B. gracilis was first described and a little later, in 1688, the plant which is widely grown today under the name of B. acutifolia was collected in Jamaica.

Opposite: 'Sugar Candy', a magnificent example of the large-flowered, double, tuberous begonias

The Iron Cross begonia, *B. masoniana*, has deeply puckered leaves with distinctive markings

The first begonia to arrive in Britain was *B. nitida* (minor), which was sent to Kew in 1777. From then on, new species began to reach Britain and Europe in ever increasing numbers. In 1804, *B. evansiana* (now properly known as *B. grandis* subspecies *evansiana*) was introduced and was the first begonia species to be described in *Curtis's Botanical Magazine*, in 1812. In 1856, the original *B. rex* was found in Assam, India, and supposedly reached Britain by chance in an importation of orchid plants. From this, the enormous range of popular Rex cultivars has been evolved. Then in 1865, from Bolivia, came *B. pearcei*, the first of several South American tuberous species with flowers of various colours. These were immediately taken up by British and Continental nurserymen, who produced hybrids which were the forerunners of our modern giant-flowered tuberous begonias.

Another important introduction was the Brazilian *B. semperflorens*, a pink-flowered shrubby plant, found in 1878. Its cultivars are now grown in huge numbers for summer bedding. The year 1880 saw the arrival of *B. socotrana*, a winter-flowering bulbous species from the Indian Ocean island of Socotra, off the coast of Somalia. This was used by French growers to produce the Lorraine series of winter-flowering plants and by English hybridizers for the larger-flowered Optima or Hiemalis group. Although both were grown extensively before the Second World War, they have been largely replaced today by the Rieger begonias, developed in West Germany from 1955, which are among our most popular houseplants.

In 1948, *B. bowerae* was discovered in Mexico and was introduced into Britain in 1952 by Maurice Mason, a noted amateur grower from Norfolk. This species has been a parent of numerous hybrids, often collectively called eyelash begonias because of the prominent whiskers edging the leaves, which have proved very amenable as houseplants. Mr Mason was also responsible for the introduction from Malaya of *B. masoniana*, known as the Iron Cross begonia owing to the dark pattern on the leaves.

Since 1945, a large number of new species have been discovered and many hundreds of hybrids have been raised, mainly in the USA, although amateurs like the late Mr Macintyre of Liverpool have helped to maintain the expertise of British growers in the field. The American Begonia Society, founded in 1932, has been the agency for the introduction of many of the new species, collected all over the world. In addition, the society operates a registration list, which records the name and parentage of new hybrids of any significant interest, along similar lines to *Sander's List of Orchid Hybrids*.

DISTRIBUTION AND CLASSIFICATION

Species of begonia are found in Mexico, Central and South America, Africa and over a large area of the Far East, usually in quite localized areas for a particular species. They occur in tropical and temperate climes and at various elevations and, therefore, temperature ranges. This wide distribution in nature, with obviously a diverse set of environmental conditions, has resulted in such varied habits of growth among the species that it is difficult to give general advice on cultivation to cover them all. Add to this the numerous hybrids that have been made and the

picture becomes even more confused. However, things are not as bad as they look and it is perfectly feasible to break down the genus into groups requiring similar treatment.

As will be explained, these artificial divisions should also help us decide which plants may be grown where. For instance, we all know what a riot of colour can be obtained in the garden by bedding out the modern varieties of B. *semperflorens*, which seem to grow in sun or shade with very little attention. The same sort of position, though, would be useless for the beautiful foliage begonias in the rhizomatous group, which need shade and protection from the vagaries of the elements to preserve the velvety texture of the leaves. However, with such an enormous range of plants to choose from, we can find a begonia which can be grown in almost any situation.

Several classifications have been proposed, but for the purposes of this book the genus has been divided into six sections (with corresponding chapters), which seem to be the most practical for defining cultural needs and methods. These are as follows:

Rhizomatous (p.23): striking foliage plants, often with the bonus of flowers, including the B. rex cultivars and species like B. *bowerae* and B. *manicata*.

Cane-stemmed (p.30): tall plants valued equally for flowers and leaves, the latter resembling angel's wings or being lobed and wavy.

Tuberous (p.35): plants with large single or double flowers in late summer, the favourites at flower shows; together with Multiflora plants for bedding and species such as B. *sutherlandii*.

Fibrous-rooted (p.42): bushy plants grown mainly for flowers, including B. *metallica* and B. *haageana* (*scharffii*); and also B. *semperflorens* cultivars for summer bedding.

Winter-flowering (p.49): Lorraine and Rieger begonias with showy flowers.

Miscellaneous (p.51): plants which do not fit easily into any of these categories and require special conditions.

Where appropriate, a selection of species and hybrids within the group is given at the end of the chapter. Most are easy to grow and all are in cultivation in Britain.

Opposite: A variety, probably *nigramarga*, of the original eyelash begonia, B. *bowerae*

General Cultivation

A small mixed collection of begonias which will give colour throughout the year is easy to look after, whether in the greenhouse, conservatory or home. This chapter examines the various uses of begonias and their cultivation requirements generally, including compost, watering, feeding, temperature and light. Further details of the needs of specific groups will be found in the chapters devoted to them.

IN A GREENHOUSE

In a greenhouse where a minimum winter temperature of 45°F (7°C) is maintained, the majority of the plants described in this book can be grown. During the summer months, begonias under glass need shading of some sort, either the kind which is painted on to the outside of the glass, or tinted plastic sheet or netting fixed inside. The shading also helps to keep the temperature down in very hot weather. Air should be admitted freely whenever possible, not only to reduce the temperature but to give good air circulation around the plants and reduce the chance of infection by botrytis or powdery mildew. This is particularly important with the large-flowered tuberous varieties. A high humidity is not essential for begonias in a cool greenhouse and it is not recommended to spray them as a regular routine, since water remaining around the lower stems for a long time can cause rotting, especially in the rhizomatous types. It is, however, very good practice to flood the pots with water occasionally in the summer. This will remove most of the salts that build up in the compost, particularly in hard water areas, and help to prevent souring of the compost and subsequent loss of roots.

Begonias, on the whole, prefer slightly acid conditions. A suitable compost for most purposes is made up of equal parts by volume of John Innes No. 2 potting compost and sphagnum moss peat, with half a part of coarse grit or perlite to keep the mixture open and free-draining. The plants appreciate fairly frequent potting on or repotting, using this mixture. Young plants in 2 in. (5 cm) pots may be potted first into $3\frac{1}{2}$ in. (9 cm) pots, then three months later into $5\frac{1}{2}$ in. (14 cm) half-pots. Subsequently, at intervals of about six months in spring and early autumn, they are repotted by taking the plant out of the pot and dividing it if necessary, removing most of the old compost and returning the

The large-flowered tuberous begonias need plenty of room and are probably best grown in a greenhouse

plant to the same pot with fresh compost. A $5\frac{1}{2}$ in. (14 cm) pot gives a plant quite large enough for most purposes, the spread of a rhizomatous begonia being about 1 ft (30 cm), although if a show specimen is required, the plant may be potted on in stages into a much larger pot.

Watering is, of course, dependent on the size of plant relative to its container and on temperature, humidity and light. Begonias should be allowed to get fairly dry between waterings. Many will show their need for water by drooping stems and this is the time to soak the compost; after an hour or so, the plant should return to its normal upright appearance. In a cool greenhouse, growth is most active from April to November and the plants require additional feeding, say at every third watering. A high potash feed is best and a liquid fertilizer such as Tomorite gives very good results with both foliage and flowering begonias. During winter, when growth is at a minimum or even at a complete standstill, watering should be reduced accordingly and no feeding is necessary.

It is possible to find positions to suit particular plants in the greenhouse. Generally, the cane-stemmed and tuberous begonias need the most light and fibrous begonias a little less, while the rhizomatous varieties require more shade, many growing extremely well under the greenhouse staging.

In a warmer greenhouse, kept at about 55°F (13°C) minimum, begonias from more exotic sources may be grown, together with many of the others suitable for a cool greenhouse. The latter would as a result have a longer growing season and need more frequent watering and feeding. Higher humidity is more acceptable with the higher temperature, but care should still be taken not to overwater. Under these conditions it is advisable to increase the amount of drainage material in the compost to admit more air to the roots.

IN A CONSERVATORY

A north-facing conservatory is ideal for begonias and a mixed collection may be grown in much the same way as in a cool greenhouse, repotting at similar intervals, watering only when dry and feeding regularly during the summer. Plants can easily be stood outside in the garden to flush out excess salts from the compost with a hosepipe.

In conservatories that do not face north, shading and ventilation will have to be introduced to reduce the light intensity and temperature sufficiently. If the temperature is likely to exceed 90°F (32°C) or direct sunlight cannot be excluded, then begonias (and in fact most other plants) can be ruled out.

IN THE HOME

Indoors, the problem is not so much high light levels as shade and it is here that begonias prove so useful, particularly the rhizomatous kinds. These will grow in quite shady positions, but not of course in the half-dark. A north window is a good place and can be used for rhizomatous and fibrous begonias. East or west aspects will accommodate fibrous and cane begonias and should afford enough light for them to flower well. However, a south-

'Fairylight', a large-flowered, double, tuberous begonia of the picotee type, having a thin edge of colour to the petals

facing window is not suitable, unless there is substantial shading to protect the plants from direct sunlight through the glass. Semperflorens begonias may also be grown in a light situation in the home and, if it is to their liking, will provide flowers continually. The large-flowered tuberous types may be used for temporary decoration, but need a fair amount of room and careful culture to bring them to perfection. For year-long flowers the Rieger begonias, which have been specifically developed as houseplants, are difficult to surpass.

Never place a begonia near a central heating radiator or an open fire, as this will result in brown shrivelled edges to the leaves. Similarly, avoid draughts. Begonias are not affected by central heating and temperatures within a house are generally suitable. A comfortable temperature for humans is also enjoyed by begonias. Watering and feeding should be carried out on the same principles as in a greenhouse, that is, water only when the compost in the pot is dry and give a high potash fertilizer at intervals while the plant is in active growth.

'Golden Shower', a tuberous Pendula hybrid which is ideal for a hanging basket

Some of the exotic tropical begonias may be grown in a heated terrarium, where conditions of high temperature and humidity can be achieved. Such a container, be it a modified aquarium or a purpose-built cabinet, can be used for gems like *B. versicolor*, with velvety multicoloured leaves, and the miniature *B. prismatocarpa*, with a constant display of yellow red-striped flowers. Most of these stove begonias require a much lighter, more open compost than the general range of begonias, in fact many are epiphytic or tree-dwelling in the their natural habitats. A mixture of live sphagnum moss and leafmould suits the majority, with a layer of pea shingle underneath to ensure adequate drainage, together with a fairly constant temperature of around 70°F (21°C).

IN THE GARDEN

The cultivars of B. *semperflorens* are among the finest plants available for summer bedding. Raised from seed under glass in the early part of the year (see pp. 21–2) they will flower continuously from the moment they are planted out in May until the first frosts of autumn. At the end of the season, perhaps in September, any particularly good plants may be lifted and potted, to grow as flowering houseplants during the winter.

The Multiflora tuberous hybrids also make excellent bedding plants and will give hundreds of flowers in a wide range of colours all summer. They are raised from seed with heat in the same way as the Semperflorens begonias, but are lifted in the autumn and stored through the winter. The next spring they may be started into growth again and planted out in the garden or used as summer-flowering pot plants in the home.

Under similar conditions outside, some of the fibrous begonias do very well, either as dot plants among bedding begonias or in a container on a patio. The best for this purpose include B. *incarnata*, B. *acutifolia* and B. 'Ingramii', which all form nice shrubby plants some 2 ft (60 cm) high. Other glossy-leaved fibrous begonias may be worth trying here. Semperflorens and Multiflora begonias are also excellent in containers, together with the tuberous Pendula hybrids in hanging baskets. For sunnier parts of the garden, the large-flowered tuberous begonias can be impressive in flower, but do need a little attention with staking and removing old blooms.

One tuberous begonia that does not need to be lifted and stored is B. *grandis* subspecies *evansiana*. This is completely hardy in the southern half of Britain and, if planted in a garden border, will emerge in May to make a plant 2 ft (60 cm) high, with many bright pink flowers in August and September. A white form is also grown.

Propagation

Begonias are propagated by one of four methods, namely stem cuttings, division, leaf cuttings and from seed.

STEM CUTTINGS

Fibrous-rooted, cane-stemmed and tuberous begonias may be increased by stem cuttings. All the fibrous-rooted begonias are easily propagated by cuttings taken during spring and summer and rooted in pots of a peat and sand mixture in the greenhouse, conservatory or indoors without any additional heat. If a heated propagator is available, this can be done at any time of year. For the best results, cuttings are taken from shoots near the base of the plant and should be 3–6 in. (7.5–15 cm) long, cut with a sharp knife between two nodes. Remove the lower two or three leaves and insert the cutting to about half its length into a mixture of equal parts of sharp sand and moss peat in a small pot (see figure 1). Gently water the cutting in and then treat it as an ordinary plant, allowing the pot to become almost dry before watering. There is no need to enclose the pot in a polythene bag; in fact this is more likely to cause the cutting to rot. Cuttings should root in about three weeks during the summer and may then be transferred to $3\frac{1}{2}$ in. (9 cm) pots, using the standard compost (see p.12). Many begonia cuttings will root in jars of water, but the new plant tends to suffer more of a check to the root system when potted on than when potted on from a small pot of peat and sand mixture.

Figure 1: stem cutting of a fibrous-rooted begonia

With cane-stemmed begonias, very soft stem cuttings from the top 6 in. (15 cm) of the plant are used, or the side shoots that break from cut-back canes in spring. These root easily if treated in the same way as for fibrous-rooted begonias, in particular making sure that plenty of air circulates around them.

With tuberous begonias, surplus shoots arising from the base of the tubers in their earlier stages of growth may be taken off and used as cuttings in spring. The shoots are easily broken off with a sideways pressure of your thumb when they are about 3 in. (7.5 cm) tall. They can then be dusted with flowers of sulphur or rinsed with a fungicide and potted individually into 3 in. (7.5 cm) pots, to grow on and produce new tubers by the autumn. Ordinary stem cuttings, of the same type as for fibrous-rooted begonias, can also be taken during the summer, to root and produce new tubers by the autumn.

DIVISION

Straightforward division in spring or summer of multiple-stemmed fibrous or cane-stemmed begonias is quite feasible. Rhizomatous begonias which have formed a mat of rhizome over the surface may also be divided, although the best method for these and the Rex begonias is leaf cuttings, which develop into better-shaped plants.

Division is probably the easiest way to propagate the winter-flowering Rieger begonias. It should be done in May and June, when the longer hours of daylight and rising temperatures give the best conditions for building up a strong plant. The old plant is tipped out of its pot, revealing a number of new growths around the base of the stems, at or just below soil level. If the parent plant is a commercially produced one, the centre of the rootball will probably be enclosed by a small lattice-work plastic pot left in by the grower. This may be eased off after rubbing away the fibrous roots, allowing the new basal growths to be gently teased out from the clump, often with some roots already formed. Growths of 3–4 in. (7.5–10 cm) in length are suitable for 3 in. (7.5 cm) pots and should be potted individually in a mixture of peat and sand. Kept in a lightly shaded, airy position, they should be firmly rooted in three to four weeks. They may then be potted on into larger pots of a rich open compost, made up of leafmould, moss peat and John Innes No. 3 in equal parts, with some coarse grit or perlite to provide extra drainage. With their succulent stems and leaves, Rieger begonias do not like their feet constantly in water.

19

Leaf cuttings are an easy method of increasing Rex begonias

LEAF CUTTINGS

Rhizomatous and Rex begonias are increased by leaf cuttings, a single leaf producing many new plants. A mature, but not half-dead, leaf is selected and its stem cut to a length of 2–3 in. (5–7.5 cm). This is then planted in a small pot of peat and sand mixture to about half its length, so that the leaf sits like a flag in the pot (see figure 2). Keep it watered, in an airy atmosphere in the home or greenhouse, and it should root in summer after about two weeks. Two or three weeks later, plantlets will start to push up through the surface of the soil from the bottom of the stem. When they have made a couple of leaves each, the leaf with its plantlets should be tipped out of the pot and the clump of little plantlets carefully teased apart and potted individually into 2 in. (5 cm) pots to grow on. As well as being produced from the bottom of the cut stem, growths sometimes occur along the length of the leaf stem and from the surface of the leaf, particularly at the sinus – the junction of leaf and stem.

There are two other methods of taking leaf cuttings. The first is to peg an entire leaf flat on the surface of a tray of peat and sand compost and cut across the main veins (see figure 3). Young plants appear after a few weeks from the cuts and may be detached and

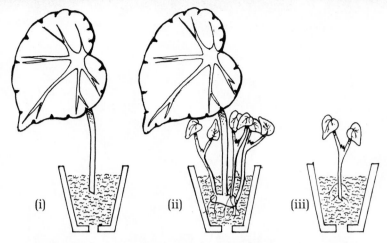

Figure 2: (i) leaf cutting of a rhizomatous begonia, (ii) young plants growing from the base; and (iii) potted separately

Figure 3: plantlets developing from cuts in a leaf

potted separately. The second is to cut the leaf into small wedges about 1 in. (2.5 cm) long. These are inserted vertically to half their depth in rows in a pot of compost, each to make its set of plantlets. Both methods produce a large number of plants, but are best carried out with a bottom heat of 65–75°F (18–24°C), as at lower temperatures the leaves tend to rot away before developing plantlets.

SEED

Seed, if obtainable, is an obvious way of producing new plants. It is the usual method for the Semperflorens and Multiflora begonias, carried out early in the year, in February. Prepare a compost of moss peat and coarse sand and fill a tray or pan about three quarters full with the mixture. Cover this with a layer of silver sand about $\frac{1}{4}$ in. (0.5 cm) deep. Firm the surface lightly and water with a fine rose, using a fungicide such as Benlate or Nimrod-T, to eliminate any fungus spores from the compost. The very fine seed is then dusted on to the surface and the tray or pan enclosed in a clear polythene bag or put into a propagator with a

Semperflorens begonias are raised from seed and flower throughout the summer

bottom heat of 70°F (21°C). Do not cover with newspaper as begonia seed needs light for germination. Seed begins to germinate within two weeks. When the seedlings have made their third leaf, they may be carefully transplanted into pans, about $\frac{1}{2}$ in. (1cm) apart, using the same peat and sand compost, and should be kept in the same conditions for the first few days, then hardened off by slowly reducing the temperature and gradually admitting more air over a couple of weeks. Once the temperature has been reduced to about 60°F (15°C), the seedlings may be grown without the protection of a propagator or bag. When they are about 2 in. (5 cm) tall, they are potted separately into 3 in. (7.5 cm) pots, using a mixture of two parts of moss peat and one part of John Innes No.2, and grown on under normal conditions in the greenhouse or home.

Rhizomatous Begonias

The rhizomatous group of begonias contains probably the largest number of species and hybrids grown at the present time, even if we exclude the numerous Rex begonias. They are characterized by the formation of a thickened stem called a rhizome, which may creep and branch over the surface, or in some cases just below soil level, rooting as it grows, while in some of the larger species it becomes upright and self-supporting. The leaf stalks and flower stems arise directly from the rhizome and the general habit is to make a symmetrical mound of leaves. The size of the leaves varies from 1 in. to 1 ft (2.5–30 cm) or more across and they come in very diverse shapes and colours, many with an iridescent sheen to the upper surface.

Although the foliage is the chief attraction, these begonias have the bonus of pretty flowers. The flower stems of species with prostrate rhizomes, like *B. bowerae*, grow up through the leaves to bear nodding racemes of pink or white flowers in late winter and early spring, lasting for three to four weeks. Those with upright rhizomes, such as *B. manicata*, produce flower spikes from the upper parts of the rhizome and hold the massive sprays of flowers well above the foliage, again usually early in the year. Other species, mainly of African origin, have yellow flowers for much of the year, but are generally more tender than the well-known Mexican species and their hybrids.

The first rhizomatous begonias to be introduced were tall plants 3–4 ft (90 cm–1.2 m) high and included the easily grown *B. heracleifolia* and *B. manicata* from Mexico. The latter is still widely cultivated, for even a two-year old plant may reach 2 ft (60 cm) across and 3 ft (90 cm) high and is a most impressive sight when carrying the numerous dense panicles of bright pink flowers.

The discovery of *B. bowerae* in Mexico in 1948 heralded an explosion of hybrids. The species itself is a miniature low-growing plant with a prostrate branching rhizome, from which the leaves arise on 4 in. (10 cm) stems. An inch or so (2.5 cm) long, the oval, waxy, bright green leaves have black "stitching" round the edges and a fringe of strong white hairs, giving rise to the common name of eyelash begonia (see p.57). The name is applied to the many hundreds of hybrids now in cultivation which have *B. bowerae* blood (or should we say chlorophyll?) in their ancestry.

Generally, these begonias require subdued light and certainly

Begonia manicata, one of the first rhizomatous begonias to be introduced, in 1842

should be shielded from direct sunlight. Too bright a light results in yellowed hard-textured foliage and rather small plants and leaves, while too little light leads to weak elongated stems, which droop with the weight of the leaves, and a lack of flowers. The upright-rhizomed kinds as a rule need rather more light than the dwarf clump-forming types, but still not full sun. In the home, a north-facing window is ideal and, in the greenhouse or conservatory, a position under the front edge of the staging or in the shade of taller plants is suitable.

The rhizomes and stems are quite succulent, enabling the plants to dry out for short periods, and watering is only necessary when the pot is dry, at which stage it should be soaked thoroughly. This careful watering is particularly important in winter if the temperature is below 50°F (10°C). Most of the Mexican types will withstand temperatures down to 40°F (5°C), if kept fairly dry, and up to 90°F (32°C), with an optimum range of 55–70°F (13–21°C). The compost is the standard one (see p.12) and repotting at intervals of about six months is recommended. Even with such frequent repotting, additional feeding with a high potash fertilizer is beneficial. It should start a month after repotting and should be repeated at every third watering.

The rhizomatous begonias are of very easy culture and make excellent houseplants. Also rhizomatous, but demanding a little more careful treatment, are the Rex begonias, which are valued for their spectacular leaves in an enormous range of sizes and colours. The original B. rex was discovered in Assam, India, in about 1856, growing under very shady, humid conditions. It has a rather short, thick rhizome, bearing large, dark green leaves zoned with silver. In nature it tends to be deciduous, indicating the need for a winter rest period for most of the Rex begonias. The species caused a sensation when first introduced into Belgium and within a few years there were a large number of hybrids on the market. Some of these early hybrids are still much sought after, particularly the beautiful, red-velvet, plush 'Fireflush' (see p. 26) and the silvery upright-growing 'Abel Carrière'.

Since the turn of the century, myriads of cultivars have been produced and many other species have been used in breeding, to give a range of leaf colour and form that is unsurpassed in any other group of plants. Most of these modern hybrids are unnamed or, if names are used, they are rarely reliable. Rex begonias are at their best in summer, appreciating greater warmth than many of the other rhizomatous kinds, and they should have plenty of shade and regular watering and feeding at this time. Too much light is apt to turn the foliage a dull beetroot-red, while good shade brings out the almost metallic sheen that is a feature of many of them. They require the same compost as other rhizomatous begonias, with the addition of some well-rotted leafmould, which increases the amount of food available to the plants. They are gross feeders and, when growth is most active, can be given a high potash fertilizer at every other watering. Repotting at intervals of six months, in spring and early autumn, helps to encourage the formation of new roots and therefore good strong growth. Ideally, a minimum temperature of 60°F (15°C) should be maintained in winter and the plants should be kept slightly drier during the period of reduced activity in the middle of winter.

Rex begonias will thrive in the home and make very nice

Many Rex begonias are characterized by large, lop-sided, heart-shaped leaves with remarkable colouring: 'Merry Christmas' (above left); a silver-leaved hybrid (above right); and 'Fireflush' (below)

specimen plants if given the right position. This is where they will receive a moderate amount of light, say in a north-facing aspect, away from cold draughts and radiated heat from a fire or radiator, in a moderately warm room. Water them only when the compost has become fairly dry. (See also pp.2 and 20.)

The Iron Cross begonia, *B. masoniana*, needs the same sort of cultivation. It is a species in its own right, not a Rex as is often supposed, and is so distinct in leaf colour and texture that it is well worth growing.

A SELECTION OF PLANTS (excluding Rex begonias)

B. aridicaulis. Miniature Mexican species, only 4 in. (10 cm) high. Shining, sharply tapered leaves with a lighter centre. White flowers held above the leaves in June and July.

'Aruba'. About 9 in. (23 cm) high. Lobed leaves are yellow-green with black stitching round the margins. Panicles of white flowers held above the leaves in spring.

'Barbados'. Dark and light brown, variegated, velvety leaves make a mound 6 in. (15 cm) or so high. Pink flowers in spring.

'Beatrice Haddrell'. A star-leaved hybrid which originated in 1955. The very dark leaves have brilliant green centres, this colour extending partly along the veins. Bright pink flowers in spring.

'Black Velvet'. A medium-sized plant with deeply cut 3 in. (7.5 cm) leaves of very dark, plush, brown-black and some lighter brown areas in the centre. Dark pink flowers rise on tall stems from the rhizome in spring.

B. bowerae. See p.23.

'Bunchii'. Originated with a Mr Bunch in the USA. The bright green leaves have very frilled edges and the leaves completely obscure the rhizome. Panicles of pink flowers are held above the foliage. (See p.28.)

B. caroliniaefolia. Mexican species having a thick erect rhizome up to 2 ft (60 cm) tall. Large, palmately divided leaves. Leaf stems and the undersides of the leaves are covered with a brown felt. Heads of many pink flowers on tall stems in spring.

'Cathedral'. Crisped leaf edges, the undersides having curious raised areas almost like windows. Pink flowers.

'Chantilly Lace'. A dwarf hybrid of *B. bowerae*. Bright, pale green leaves with a light stitching of black round the edges. A good compact grower. Very pale pink flowers. (See p.61.)

'Chumash'. Another hybrid of *B. bowerae*, growing larger than that species, with dark lobed leaves, mottled lighter brown in the centre. A nice neat plant. Pink flowers in spring. (See p.59.)

'Cleopatra'. An old favourite among the dwarf rhizomatous begonias. Star-shaped leaves of yellow and plush brown. Profuse pink flowers. (See p.57.)

'Emerald Isle'. Some 9 in. (23 cm) tall, with bright green, round, very thick, fleshy leaves. White flowers.

'Enchantment'. A larger-growing plant, with leaves up to 6 in. (15 cm) across, edges cleft, bright green with black-brown markings. Light pink blossoms.

'Fuscomaculata'. Very large leaves from a strong rhizome. Plant is somewhat bristly. Leaves light brown-green, spattered with dark brown markings. Greenish white flowers with red spots.

B. heracleifolia. A short thick rhizome. Leaves up to 1 ft (30 cm) across, deeply notched, rich green, black-bronze towards the edges. Upper surface of the leaves

'Bunchii' has remarkably crisped foliage

and the stems are set with white hairs. Heavy clusters of pink flowers February to April. From Mexico.

'Jamaica'. One of a series of dwarf rhizomatous begonias. Attains a height of 6 in. (15 cm), with small green leaves covered by a network of dark brown.

'Little Darling'. Forms a dwarf mound, 6 in. (15 cm) tall, of almost black leaves with bright green blotches between the veins. A good complementary plant to 'Tiger Paws'. Pink-white flowers.

B. manicata. Strong upright-rhizomed species from Mexico. Large, fleshy green leaves, with a collar of red bristles on the stem just below the leaf. Tall stems with panicles of pink flowers in spring. There are also crested leaf and variegated forms. (See p. 24.)

B. masoniana. Strong plant from Malaya. Leaves large, rounded, puckered, eau-de-nil green, with a contrasting central marking of black-brown. Greenish white flowers with dark red bristles on the back. (See p.8.)

B. mazae. A dwarf Mexican species with a trailing, red and white rhizome. Satiny leaves are shaded green and bronze, with paler veins in the centre. Pink flowers in spring.

'Norah Bedson'. Pale brown-green, fairly rounded leaves covered with a network of dark brown. To 9 in. (23 cm) tall. Pink flowers in late winter to early spring.

B. pustulata. Mexican species with a rambling tendency. Leaves are dark emerald-green with silver veins. The subspecies *argentea* has plush, dark green leaves, puckered, richly variegated with silver.

'Queen of Olympus'. Growing to 6 in. (15 cm) high. The 2 in. (5 cm) leaves are a metallic silver, bordered with olive-green.

'Raquel Wood'. Hybrid of *B. manicata*. Upright rhizome bearing mid-green lobed leaves marked with black-brown round the edges. Dark rose-pink flowers in spring held well above the foliage.

'Royal Lustre'. A miniature plant, the leaves being variegated with olive-green, emerald-green and metallic-looking gun-metal.

'Sweet Magic'. Very large, spiralled leaves in shades of mahogany and green. White flowers tinged with pink.

'Tiger Paws'. A very popular dwarf hybrid forming a mound of small leaves chequered in yellow and light brown. Masses of white flowers held over the foliage in spring. (See pp. 59.)

28

A wide range of leaf shapes and colours, often with a metallic sheen, is to be found among the rhizomatous begonias: 'Norah Bedson' (above left); *B. pustulata argentea* (above right); and 'Queen of Olympus' (below)

Cane-stemmed Begonias

The cane-stemmed begonias are probably best known from two very old hybrids, 'President Carnot' and 'Lucerna', which date from the 1890s and are still frequently seen as houseplants and in greenhouses. They are similar in habit, forming tall, stout, upright stems, often reaching 5–6 ft high (1.5–1.8 m) and rarely branching, with large leaves in the shape of angel's wings, green spotted with silver on the upper surface and deep red on the underside. Large drooping umbels of flowers are produced from the leaf axils throughout the year, pink in 'Lucerna' and a much darker colour in 'President Carnot'. The male flowers soon drop, but the female flowers with their coloured seed pods persist on the plant for some time.

Unlike most other begonias, the cane-stemmed types should have as much light as possible, short of scorching the foliage, in order to maintain the colour of the leaves and keep the distance between nodes on the stems as short as possible. Even so, they do grow very tall, but are stiff enough not to require staking. At some time, though, they will need to be cut back. If they are just beheaded or stopped, by pinching off the top of the stem or cane, the new growths generally form from a couple of joints immediately below the top, making the plant no shorter. The canes should therefore be cut down to within two or three nodes above the soil surface and will then break from these low nodes to form better-shaped plants. This is best carried out in spring. Any further pruning to induce more branches should again be done after only a few joints have been made.

An established plant will produce from below soil level very strong, suckering shoots, which grow at an amazing rate, hence the name cane begonia. Because of this rapid growth, a large pot is required, preferably of clay to give the extra weight for stability, and a rich compost consisting of equal parts by volume of John Innes No. 3 potting compost and sphagnum moss peat. After having been potted for six weeks or so, additional regular feeding with a high potash fertilizer is appreciated. Repotting should be undertaken each year in spring and again in early autumn.

A common occurrence with the cane-stemmed begonias is the loss of the lower leaves, resulting in tall bare stems with a few

Opposite: The popular 'Lucerna' flowers mainly in late spring and summer

leaves and flowers at the top. This is usually caused by over-watering. The pots should be allowed to get fairly dry before watering, since a sodden compost will destroy the fine hair roots on which the plant depends. Similarly, if a plant has been in the same pot for a long time, the soil may have become so compacted that air is excluded from the roots and it can be difficult for water to penetrate the centre of the root ball. The condition is often indicated by browning of the leaf tips and curling of the leaves before they fall. The best remedy is to take the begonia out of its container, remove as much of the old soil as possible from the root ball and repot into fresh compost. A begonia which is starved in this way is especially vulnerable to attack by powdery mildew, but repotting should stop the fungus spreading further.

So far we have discussed the taller-growing cane begonias, derived from the Brazilian species B. coccinea and B. maculata, which are very good houseplants if there is enough room. Other species and hybrids are more modest in growth and more easily accommodated indoors. Many of these are being grown now, sadly often un-named. They have the same basic habit of growth as 'Lucerna', but attain a height of only 2–4 ft (60 cm–1.2 m). The flower colours vary from white through pink to scarlet and sometimes orange and all have angel wing leaves, some plain green, others silver-spotted. A particularly good one is 'Lucerna Amazon', a much-branched shrub up to about 3 ft (90 cm) tall. It has the typical silver-spotted leaves, 3 in. (7.5 cm) or so long, and constantly bears bright, pink-red, drooping heads of flowers from almost every leaf axil. About half this height is 'Medora', another freely branching shrub. The small pointed leaves with jagged edges are dark green with silver spots and clusters of small pink-white flowers hang from the leaf axils throughout the summer.

A number of cane-stemmed begonias have pendulous stems, rather than the normal stiff upright growth, and make excellent plants for hanging baskets. 'Orange Rubra' is a good example, with light green crinkle-edged leaves, silver-spotted, and bunches of orange and white flowers. They need the same culture as the upright growers.

Finally, there are the Superba begonias, originally developed in California in 1926 from B. aconitifolia and 'Lucerna'. They are medium-growing plants with lobed wavy leaves, generally dark green with silver splashing and streaking on the upper surface. The new foliage emerges light pink. They are very floriferous, with showy bunches of white or pink flowers. The older kinds tend to become dormant during the winter months, a habit attributed to B. aconitifolia, but more recent cultivars from the USA hold their leaves much better and have a wider range of leaf

Above left: *Begonia coccinea* may grow up to 10ft (3m) tall and flowers throughout the year
Right: the silver spots on the foliage of 'Orange Rubra' often disappear with age
Below: 'Lucerna Amazon', a smaller-growing cane begonia which is an excellent houseplant

The Superba hybrids are distinguished from other cane begonias by the serrated leaves

colours. Like most cane begonias, they like a winter temperature of 50°F (10°C) and are best repotted in spring and autumn.

A SELECTION OF PLANTS

B. albo-picta. A free-branching species from Brazil, with elliptic leaves 2 by 1 in. (5 x 2.5 cm), green, covered with silver-white spots. Greenish-white flowers hang from the leaf axils. Small-growing, to 2 ft (60 cm). There is a pink-flowered form. (See p.60.)

B. coccinea. Very tall, stout canes with sharply pointed 6 by 2 in. (15 x 5 cm) leaves. Flowers are deep pink in large clusters from the leaf axils. The angel wing leaves are plain green. From Brazil. (See p.33.)

'Lucerna'. See p.30.

'Lucerna Amazon'. See p.32.

'Medora'. See p.32.

'Orange Rubra'. See p.32.

'President Carnot'. See p.30.

Superba. See p.32.

B. 'Esther Albertine'. Much divided, silver-speckled leaves, light pink flowers produced almost continuously.

B. 'Irene Nuss'. Velvety green foliage and very large trusses of coral pink flowers.

B. 'Sophie Cecile'. Deeply lobed leaves streaked with silver and lots of pink flowers.

Tuberous Begonias

Following the introduction to Britain in the 1860s of half a dozen species of tuberous begonia from South America, the ancestors of our modern range of hybrids were developed. The first of these, in 1869, was 'Sedenii', named after its raiser, John Seden, of the Chelsea nurserymen Veitch and Sons. Others followed in quick succession from many growers, both in Britain and on the Continent. In 1901 the firm of Blackmore and Langdon was founded near Bristol and soon became renowned for its collection of tuberous begonias.

These are the strong upright-growing begonias seen so often on show benches throughout the country and tended with such loving care to bloom in the late summer. There is now a vast range of hybrids, with the large single and double forms predominating (see pp. 6, 13, 37, 64). The singles are brilliantly coloured in red, pink, white, yellow or orange, some with the edges of the petals ruffled and crinkled. In addition, the Marginata types have frilled margins of a different colour from the base colour of the flower, while the Cristata types have even more crisped or fringed petals. The giant-flowered doubles are usually divided into two groups – camellia-flowered, with large open flowers, and rosebud, with a tight centre resembling, as the name suggests, a rosebud. The same wide variety of colours is available as in the singles, and some have ruffled edges to the petals. It is best to choose plants by referring to the catalogues of specialist growers.

Developed along with these were the tuberous Pendula hybrids, which have long pendulous stems and make extremely showy plants for hanging baskets. The display of flowers lasts all through the summer and they come in the same range of colours and variation of form as the upright-growing plants (see pp. 16 and 39). A distinct drooping kind is B. 'Bertinii', which is very close to B. boliviensis, one of the original species, and carries quantities of single red flowers.

The Multiflora tuberous hybrids are now becoming popular as outdoor bedding plants for summer, particularly the Nonstop varieties (see p.38). They are readily grown from seed to flower in the first season and they form tubers in the open ground which may be stored over the winter for use in subsequent years. They also make excellent houseplants during the summer.

All tuberous begonias may be grown from seed (see pp. 21–2), except the named forms, which are propagated from stem cuttings and usually purchased as tubers from a specialist nursery. When buying tubers, choose only those that are firm, not shrivelled, and free from any soft patches. For early flowers, the dormant tubers should be started into growth in February, at a temperature of 60–65°F (15–18°C) in trays of compost. A suitable compost is made up of equal volumes of John Innes No. 2 and moss peat. Tubers should be set in the trays a few inches apart, making sure that the top of the tuber is covered with compost, since roots are produced all over the top surface of the tuber. The top is the concave side and particular care must be taken that they are not planted upside down. They are then gently watered in, preferably using a liquid fungicide in the water, and covered with a sheet of newspaper. Should heat not be available, the same procedure may be followed to start them in a cold greenhouse at the end of April, although of course the first flowers will be a little later.

In a few days, new shoots will begin to emerge on some of the tubers. Sprouting is often very erratic, young tubers seeming to give quicker results. Flower colour also appears to have an influence and darker colours start into growth slightly sooner than the pale colours and white. Once the new pink shoots are visible, remove the paper covering, but keep the tray of tubers well shaded. In another week or two, roots will have developed and leaves will be forming. The tubers can then be potted individually into 4 in. (10 cm) pots of the same compost, potting them fairly loosely in these first pots. Handle them carefully, since the new growths and roots are very brittle and easily broken. Keep these pots well shaded and widely spaced, to allow free circulation of air around the plants. Water very carefully to avoid the possibility of the stems rotting at soil level. It is a good idea to add a liquid fungicide to the water.

At this stage, it is necessary to decide whether the plant is to be grown for a few large flowers or many smaller ones. Often, when the tubers have started into growth, more than one sprout appears from the top of the tuber and, if several stems are allowed to grow on, quite a number of flowers will be produced. For the maximum size of flower, therefore, some of the shoots should be removed when they are about 3 in. (7.5 cm) tall, to leave just one strong growth. These surplus shoots can be used as cuttings (see p.19).

When the plants have reached a height of 8–9 in. (20–23 cm), it is time to pot them on into 6–7 in. (15–18 cm) pots, using a mixture of two parts by volume of John Innes No. 3 and one part of moss peat, plus some extra coarse grit for good drainage. (Many growers have their own special compost for their begonias and experiment to find the best mixture.) The pots should now be

'Zoe Colledge', one of the spectacular forms of the giant-flowered, double, tuberous begonias

placed on the greenhouse staging, with plenty of space between them to ensure adequate circulation of fresh air around the plants, and as much air as possible should be admitted to the greenhouse. They should be kept in good light, but shaded from the direct rays of the sun. Water them only when they are completely dry and then soak the compost thoroughly. After two or three weeks, begin weekly additional feeding with a high potash fertilizer. High nitrogen fertilizers are not advisable, since they induce excessive new growth which tends to be rather soft and liable to attack by botrytis or powdery mildew.

As the plants grow, the stems and large flowers need to be staked. They should be carefully tied in to split canes, using a

Above: Pendula hybrids give a profusion of bloom in summer and autumn
Opposite: Tuberous Nonstop begonias are delightful bedding plants for the garden

fairly wide material like raffia to avoid the tie cutting into the stem. To obtain the largest flowers, buds should be removed so that only the biggest ones are left; these should be about 1 in. (2.5 cm) six weeks before the date desired for the bloom to be open. If a larger number of smaller flowers is wanted, then the only disbudding required is to remove the two side buds from each set of three. The flower stems usually produce buds in sets of three, the centre one being the male flower and the two side ones being merely secondary.

When flowering is over, watering should be reduced to almost nothing and the old leaves and debris removed as they fall, until the main stems finally fall off the tubers. When dry, the tubers should be taken out of the pots and most of the old compost cleaned away. They are dusted with flowers of sulphur and stored in a box of dry peat at a temperature of about 40°F (5°C) until the next season. One or two plants could be grown in the house, but since they take up a lot of room, a greenhouse is really necessary to grow any number.

Multiflora, Pendula and Bertinii begonias need similar treatment when grown as pot plants, but staking and disbudding are not required.

As bedding plants for the garden, Multifloras may be either raised from seed, or started as tubers in the same way as the large-flowered begonias. They are potted into $3\frac{1}{2}$ in. (9 cm) pots and kept under glass until the danger of frost is past, when they may be planted out. They can remain outside until the autumn and are then lifted and put into trays for the foliage to die down. The small tubers are stored through the winter in the same way as the others.

Among the tuberous-rooted species are some extremely good plants. One such is B. sutherlandii, a low-growing plant from Natal, South Africa, where it blooms from December to February. As a cultivated plant in Britain, it will start to make growth from the tuber at about the end of March. It forms a bush with red arching stems, bearing small, light green, serrated leaves with a metallic sheen, and produces myriads of small orange flowers constantly from early summer until the end of October. As the plant begins to die down, tiny miniature tubers, called bulbils, are formed in many of the leaf axils. These may be collected and stored like the tubers to plant the next season, when they will make flowering plants. Although B. sutherlandii is found in damp shady sites in its native habitat, it seems to like a fairly light position when grown in pots and will accept quite dry air. A popular houseplant, it is, however, very susceptible to powdery mildew and regular treatment with a fungicide is a wise precaution.

Another begonia that produces bulbils in the leaf axils is B. grandis subspecies evansiana. This originates from China and Japan and is completely hardy in the south of England. Tubers may be planted permanently in the garden and soon make a nice clump if the bulbils are lightly raked in after falling in the autumn. New growth appears in late spring to form a branching, 2 ft (60 cm) high plant, with green leaves overcast with a metallic sheen, red on the undersides, some 4 in. (10 cm) across. In a sunny situation the plant is somewhat shorter and the leaves are golden green with a metallic lustre, although it succeeds equally in shade and in almost any soil. In August, the bright pink flowers are produced on stems clear of the leaves, usually in pairs, and last until the plant begins to die down in October (see p.63). A white-flowered form is also in cultivation.

Begonia sutherlandii, widely grown as a summer-flowering windowsill plant, may be placed outdoors in a shady spot when in flower

Another bulbil-producing begonia is *B. gracilis* variety *martiana*. It is a Mexican plant, not as hardy as *B. grandis evansiana*, but still easy to grow. Known as the hollyhock begonia, it grows a single upright stem to a height of about 2 ft (60 cm) and bears pink flowers in pairs close to the stem, like a small hollyhock. The leaves gradually change shape as they go up the stem, being rounded near the base and becoming long and pointed at the top. Winter is the dormant period for this plant, so treatment is much the same as for *B. sutherlandii*.

Very few of the other tuberous species are seen today, although the scarlet-flowered *B. boliviensis* is sometimes grown. It forms slender stems which are upright at first, then tend to droop over as they attain their height of 2–3 ft (6–90 cm). The leaves are long, serrated and very pointed, contrasting well with the drooping panicles of flowers. Another species, *B. froebelii*, carries its scarlet flowers in mid-winter on long stems, above velvety green heart-shaped leaves. Finally, *B. cinnabarina* makes a small bush of zig-zag stems bearing lobed, serrated, light green, hairy leaves and produces cinnabar-red flowers in summer. There are a number of other very desirable tuberous species, but they appear to be quite difficult to obtain.

41

Fibrous-rooted Begonias

The fibrous-rooted begonias are usually bushy and freely branching, producing multiple growths from the base, and make pleasant symmetrical plants. Their leaves are very diverse in size and texture, as is the height of the plants. Two of the best known species are *B. metallica* and *B. haageana*, both with hairy leaves and both originating from Brazil. A well-branched shrub up to 5 ft (1.5 m) tall, *B. metallica* has serrated leaves 6 by 3 in. (15 x 7.5 cm), which are green and hairy, with a metallic bronze lustre. The flowers form in large clusters from the leaf axils and are blush-white, thickly set with red hairs on the back of the petals. It is free-flowering throughout most of the year and easy to grow. Similar in size and manner of growth, *B. haageana* (*scharffii*) has broader red-brown leaves and the whole plant is covered with fine hairs. The flowers are rose-pink, borne all the year round (see p.60).

These begonias, like the vast majority of fibrous-rooted kinds, need good light, but not direct sunlight through glass. Too much light results in yellowish bleached leaves, while too little gives long drawn stems and an almost total lack of flowers. They require a temperature between 45° and 80°F (7–26°C), with around 55°F (13°C) as the optimum. Humidity need not be high, in fact fairly dry air is conducive to firm growth and good flower production. It also gives less chance for any moulds to appear, although this group of begonias is unlikely to develop powdery mildew. Water should be given only when the compost is dry, but it will be found that many plants require frequent watering, since the large amount of foliage on a plant in, say, a 5 in. (13 cm) pot will transpire a considerable amount of water. A high potash fertilizer should be given at every third watering when the plant is in active growth.

As opposed to the hairy-leaved plants, there are others with bare leaves, some of which are tough enough to be used outside in the summer, either as patio plants in pots or tubs or planted out in the border. In the open the leaves often take on a red or red-tinged colour and the flowers become much darker than similar plants grown under glass. It is, of course, necessary to take them under cover before the first frost. Plants that can be treated in this way include *B. incarnata*, *B. acutifolia* and *B.* 'Ingramii'. The showy *B. incarnata* from Mexico attains a height of 2½ ft (75 cm) or more and has smooth, shiny green leaves, sometimes just tinged red round the edges. Lots of bright pink 1 in. (2.5 cm) diameter

Begonia metallica, an old favourite as a houseplant, does well in a north-facing window

flowers with red backs are produced from the leaf axils. A generally smaller green-leaved plant, *B. acutifolia* was introduced from Jamaica in 1790. Pink buds open to produce white flowers almost the whole year. 'Ingramii', an early hybrid of *B. nitida* (*minor*) and *B. fuchsioides*, is rather like a small-leaved version of *B. incarnata*, with dark pink flowers freely borne in winter.

For growing in the cool greenhouse or indoors, there are many more fibrous-rooted begonias. From Colombia, we have *B. foliosa*, which is almost fern-like in its appearance. The long, slender, arching stems, freely branching and with many basal shoots, are clothed in tiny, toothed, oval, glossy green leaves and small white flowers hang in pairs below the stems in summer. It is a delightful hanging basket plant in a lightly shaded position in a warm room, greenhouse or conservatory. If a temperature of 55°F (13°C) can be maintained in the winter, *B. serratipetala* also makes a very impressive plant for a hanging basket. It comes from New Guinea and the dark stems carry deeply serrated leaves, 2 in. (5 cm) long, red-brown with bright pink spots, and many pink and white flowers.

There are some species like *B. chlorosticta* and *B. exotica* (*brevirimosa*) that are bushy in habit with beautifully coloured

43

foliage. Most of these, though, originate from the tropics and need high temperatures and humidity. They are best grown in a terrarium.

Included in the fibrous-rooted begonias are the popular Semperflorens or wax begonias. The original species, B. semperflorens, was introduced in 1821 from Brazil and was hybridized and selected to give an enormous range of flower colour, from white through to deep red and bicolors. Modern development of the F_1 hybrids has given plants that are easily grown from seed (see pp. 21–2) and very free-flowering in a wide variety of conditions. Grown as garden plants, they produce a remarkable display of bloom all summer and are particularly trouble-free. It is a good idea to prepare the bed or border for them by forking in some organic material like peat or garden compost, to make the soil more moisture-retentive. Space the plants about 1 ft (30 cm) apart, firm lightly and water in. Water them freely in dry weather and feed occasionally with a high potash fertilizer. They are equally happy in sun or shade.

Semperflorens begonias also make admirable houseplants. In the house they like light airy positions, not in direct sunlight. Allow them to dry out between waterings and feed with a high potash fertilizer at every third watering. Seedlings potted into 3 in. (7.5 cm) pots start to flower as soon as a few leaves have been made and, if potted on into 5 in. (13 cm) pots as they grow, will make plants 1 ft (30 cm) across and as much high, completely covered with flowers and blooming continuously. Particularly good forms may be overwintered safely at a minimum winter temperature of 50°F (10°C), provided care is taken to keep them fairly dry and to remove any debris of old leaves and flowers from within the plant stems. In spring, stem cuttings (see p.18) may be taken from such overwintered plants.

Also available are named double-flowered forms, which must be propagated by cuttings and are usually grown as pot plants. 'Gustav Lund' was the first really good double form, appearing in 1936, and has flowers like balls of pink crepe paper. It was followed by other varieties with white or red flowers. These doubles are most attractive plants and yet do not seem to have become very popular in this country.

A species closely allied to B. semperflorens is B. cucullata, also from Brazil and cultivated in exactly the same way. It is up to $2\frac{1}{2}$ ft (75 cm) tall, with bronze-green rounded leaves and a continual succession of pink flowers on 2 in. (5 cm) stems from the leaf axils.

Opposite: Organdy F_1 hybrids, just a sample of the enormous variety of Semperflorens begonias available today

Above: *Begonia fuchsioides* bears fuchsia-like flowers in winter
Below: Sometimes called the shrimp begonia, *B. glaucophylla* (*radicans*)
looks best in a hanging basket

Above: The unusual *Begonia luxurians*, from Brazil with small, creamy flowers, needs similar conditions to *B. metallica*

Below: *Begonia solananthera* is one of the few members of the genus to have scented flowers

A SELECTION OF PLANTS

B. acutifolia. See p.43.

B. angularis. Much-branched shrub with angled stems, 3 ft (90 cm) tall, with broad green leaves, widely veined silver, red on the underside. Many small white flowers in each cluster. From Brazil. (See p.61.)

B. compta. A tall-growing Brazilian species, having long, tapered, grey-green leaves with silver stripes lining the veins. Small white flowers in tight clusters.

B. cubensis. Shrubby, to 2 ft (60 cm). Dark bronze leaves with crinkled edges. White flowers are borne continuously. Needs a good light. From Cuba.

B. cucullata. See p.44.

'Druryi'. Tall, shrubby, with dark brown-green, slightly hairy leaves, maroon-red beneath. Large bunches of white flowers on long drooping stems in late summer and autumn. (See p.59.)

B. foliosa. See p.43.

B. fuchsioides. From Mexico. Stems erect, slender, 2–3 ft (60–90 cm) tall. Leaves many, smooth, tinged with red when young. Flowers pink or red, drooping. Cool airy conditions are best. (See p.46.)

B. glaucophylla (radicans). Stems very long, trailing or climbing, with glaucous green, 3 in. (7.5 cm) leaves. Flowers brick-red, borne freely all winter. Originating from Brazil, likes warmth and some sun. An excellent basket plant. (See p.46.)

B. haageana (B. scharffii). See p.42.

B. incarnata. See pp. 42–3.

'Ingramii'. See p.43.

B. listada. Upright, branching. Leaves narrow, double-pointed, with a bright yellow-green stripe down the centre. White blooms, with red hairs on the back. From Brazil. (See p.55.)

B. luxurians. Tall, upright, branching. Leaves large, very divided like palm leaves, green on top, hairy, with a small ruffle of leaves at the centre of each leaf. Flowers small, creamy, in long-stalked clusters. (See p.47.)

B. metallica. See p.42.

B. olsoniae. Compact shrubby plant from Brazil. Leaves are up to 6 in. (15 cm) across, bronze-green with yellow veins and red hairs. Grows to 2 ft (60 cm) tall. Flowers large, white.

B. polyantha. An elegant shrub of stiff, thin, green stems, red at the nodes, carrying satiny, russet-green, pointed leaves. Many upright heads of little white flowers. From Sumatra.

B. sanguinea. Shrubby, stems becoming woody with age. Smooth, shining, fleshy leaves, light brown-green above, blood-red beneath. Small white flowers in winter. From Brazil.

B. serratipetala. See p.43.

B. solananthera. A trailing plant with 2 in. (5 cm) heart-shaped pea-green leaves. Dense bunches of white flowers are produced in good light during winter and spring, which are fragrant in the morning and evening. From Brazil. (See p.47.)

Winter-flowering Begonias

In 1892 the hybrid 'Gloire de Lorraine' made its debut in France. It is a cross between *B. socotrana*, a warmth-loving bulbous species, and *B. dregei*, a semi-tuberous species from Natal. It forms a dense bush about 1 ft (30 cm) high of rounded, bright green leaves and carries broad panicles of numerous, small, white or pink flowers, held well above the leaves, from November until March. Up to the Second World War, the Lorraine begonias were used extensively for winter decoration of greenhouses and conservatories and as temporary indoor plants, but are rarely seen now. Not only do they require a winter minimum temperature of about 60°F (15°C) to succeed, but they are very susceptible to moulds like botrytis, as the cup-like leaves tend to hold water.

A parallel development to the 'Lorraine' begonias was the Optima or Hiemalis group. From the crossing of *B. socotrana* with a red-flowered tuberous hybrid in 1883 in London evolved a wide range of winter-flowering begonias. They have larger flowers and in a greater variety of colours than the Lorraine types, but are more untidy and straggly. Work on the Optima begonias, which began in 1955 in West Germany, has resulted in the Rieger begonias, with their many different flower colours, both single and double, and a vastly improved growth habit and resistance to mildew. These have virtually replaced the older winter-flowering begonias to become some of the most important products of the houseplant trade.

Rieger begonias are compact and bushy, branching freely from the base, with somewhat fleshy green or red-tinged leaves. The basal stems are often slightly swollen at or just below soil level, showing their tuberous ancestry. The plants are almost perpetual-blooming, with long racemes of flowers, up to 2 in. (5 cm) across, from the leaf axils, in white, yellow, peach, pink or red, reaching a peak of production during the winter months.

They will tolerate temperatures down to 50°F (10°C) and up to 90°F (32°C), the ideal being about 65°F (18°C), which gives plenty of flowers. At higher temperatures, with a long daylength, plants will make good leaf growth but produce few flowers. A moderate light, such as is obtained in a north window, is quite satisfactory. Watering is needed only when the pot has dried out and a high potash fertilizer should be given at every other watering to ensure continuation of flowers. Probably the most important factor in the treatment of these begonias is fresh air. Too close an environment

Rieger begonias have become some of our most popular winter-flowering houseplants

leads to static air around the plant and mildew spores can easily take hold. Should a plant become infected, it must be moved to a more airy situation and treated with a fungicide.

When Rieger begonias require repotting, after about six months, a compost of equal parts John Innes No. 3, moss peat and leafmould, with coarse grit or perlite, should be used. It is advisable to position the plant in such a way that the top of the old root ball is level with or just above the surface of the fresh compost, which will prevent water settling around the base of the stems. This precaution is necessary only with these begonias: in fact most of the other groups, particularly rhizomatous begonias, like to be repotted a little deeper in the compost each time. When the stem becomes too congested or the plant gets too straggly, it is best to start a new plant by division (see p.19).

Rieger begonias are sold as pot plants and generally bought on sight at a garden centre, florist or chain store. There are some named varieties, but these are not often seen.

Miscellaneous Begonias

There are several begonias which do not fall into any of the sections already dealt with and some of these are widely grown. Among them is a small group of semi-tuberous species, mainly from South Africa, typified by B. partita from Natal. This makes a bushy little plant about 1 ft (30 cm) high, with much-branched stems growing from a thickened, irregularly shaped base, which carry small many-lobed leaves, dark bronze-green with red stems and veins. During summer, a profusion of white flowers covers the plant and, at this time particularly, it needs a lot of light, with some sunlight in the early morning and late evening being very beneficial. As winter approaches, the plant begins to shed its leaves and smaller branches and it will then be seen that the lower part of the main stem is considerably swollen, especially near the bottom. Watering should be gradually reduced and, when quite dry, the thickened stem will be in a dormant state if the temperature is 40–50°F (4–10°C) and should be kept dry in its pot until the spring. If, however, the winter temperature is held at 60°F (15°C) or more, dormancy is not complete and the plant may well continue to grow as if it had reverted to a fibrous habit. It is probably best to give it a cool rest. After the dormant period, this begonia needs to be repotted in March, removing as much as possible of the compost. Replant into as small a pot as seems reasonable for the size of the plant, using a mixture of John Innes No. 2 potting compost and moss peat. Water moderately until the plant is making active growth and even at that stage allow the pot to dry between waterings. Feed with a high potash fertilizer at alternate waterings during the height of summer when the plant is growing freely.

Other species with a similar growth habit and requiring the same treatment include B. dregei, again from South Africa. This has small, deeply cut leaves, green with a red spot at the junction of each leaf with its stem, and bears white flowers in late summer. A rather taller plant, B. richardsiana, has bright green, very deeply incised leaves, also with a red spot at the base, and white flowers in the summer. A hybrid of B. sutherlandii and B. dregei, 'Weltoniensis' is an upright grower with light green, notched, lobed leaves on red stems. The flowers are light pink, very freely produced during the summer. It tends to shed its leaves for the winter but retain a lot of the stems, even while kept dry. In spring these

Begonia wollnyii (*B. williamsii*), an interesting trunk-forming species which is not often seen

old stems must be cut back to near the swollen base before new growth will start.

Then we have plants which form upright persistent trunk-stems, generally 1 ft (30 cm) or so high. An example is *B. wollnyii* from Mexico, which has an erect, slowly tapering stem bearing large light green leaves, splashed with silver and veined in red, very toothed and lobed. It drops all the leaves in autumn and spends the months from December to February as bare stems, during which time it should be kept dry. In March, bunches of pale pink flowers are produced from the upper parts of the bare stems before any leaves have formed. After flowering, new leaves are very quickly formed. Repotting is best carried out directly after flowering, before any new leaves have appeared. This type of begonia should be grown in good light with plenty of ventilation. The most reliable method of propagation is to detach the new growths that appear at the base of the main trunk at or near soil level and pot them separately.

Also included in this group is *B. ludwigii* from Ecuador. It carries green, soft-hairy, sharply lobed leaves from the top of its trunk, with the tip of each lobe splashed with silver and a collar of spine-like hairs at the join of the leaf stalk. If grown under ordinary greenhouse conditions at 50°F (10°C), it becomes leafless in winter and should be kept dry during this period of dormancy. However, if grown with extra lighting indoors, with a 12-hour or more daylength, it remains evergreen and needs watering at all seasons.

Of Brazilian origin is *B. olbia*, attaining a height of 3 ft (90 cm). The large, satiny, green-bronze leaves have darker sunken veins and the young leaves are frequently spotted with silver, which disappears as they mature. The undersides are bright red. Cream flowers are produced on very short stems directly from the main stems and are hidden by the foliage. A fairly shady position gives the best colour in the leaves. A rather higher temperature in winter is needed for this species and 50°F (10°C) is about as cool as it can go without damage.

A further set of plants is represented by the South American species *B. vitifolia*. This tree-like begonia grows 8–10 ft (2.5–3 m) high, very rarely branching, and forms stems up to 2 in. (5 cm) in diameter, with green, somewhat angled leaves $1\frac{1}{2}$ ft (45 cm) across, rough and slightly hairy. Large clusters of white flowers are borne on long stems from the upper leaf axils in late summer. There are several similar species, differing in the shape and texture of the leaves. Culture in pots is easy enough in the standard compost (see p. 12), but the accommodation of such a tall plant may present some problems.

The shrubby fibrous-rooted group contains one or two species that are found in very arid conditions in nature. They need extremely careful treatment in cultivation, with the maximum amount of light and as little water as possible, even in summer. One of these is the succulent *B. kellermannii* from the Guatemalan mountains, with felted, cupped, grey-green leaves and pink flowers. The Mexican *B. incana* (*peltata*) is thick-stemmed and very succulent. Leaves, stems and the greenish-white flowers are all covered with whitish wool, which is easily rubbed off. Tall and stout, usually single-stemmed, *B. venosa* has large, thick, very succulent leaves covered with a thick plush of silver hairs. Bunches of small white flowers are borne on red stems at almost any time of the year. For best results it should be given full sunlight. These plants require a much more open compost than normal, with a considerable proportion of coarse grit incorporated to reduce water retention, and they appreciate a little lime in the soil, a material which most begonias do not like.

A species recently introduced from Brazil by the American Begonia Society was given the name 'Burle Marx' until identified as *B. glaziovii*. A small shrub 2–3 ft (60–90 cm) across, it has

Begonia glaziovii, a sturdy compact plant which is easy to grow

branching stems which bear square-angled leaves 5 in. (13 cm) or more wide, coloured red and green, with a pebbly surface. Bunches of cream-white flowers appear during spring and summer. It is very easy to grow and can soon make a fine specimen plant. It will accept a wide range of light and humidity conditions and temperatures down to 40°F (4°C). Unlike other fibrous-rooted begonias, which can be propagated only by means of stem cuttings, *B. glaziovii* will produce a clump of plantlets from a leaf cutting, treated in the same way as for the rhizomatous begonias (see p.20). There are probably some other begonias with this property, such as *B. listada* and *B. exotica* (*brevirimosa*).

Opposite: *Begonia listada* is a beautiful shrubby species with a plush texture to the leaves

Diseases and Pests

DISEASES

Begonias are not prone to many diseases when grown under conditions that suit them and particularly when given plenty of fresh air. Their principal enemies are moulds of one form or another, the most common of these being powdery mildew. This can occur at any time of the year and is identified by the appearance on the leaves, and sometimes also on the stems, of grey-white powdery-looking spots, which spread and increase in number until the leaf finally drops. It is most likely to occur when the temperature is low and the humidity in the atmosphere is high and especially if a plant is starved or in need of repotting. These conditions often arise in an unheated greenhouse in the autumn: night temperatures may still be relatively warm at about 50°F (10°C), but cool enough to create high humidity and condensation of water on the plants after a warm day, particularly if there is insufficient ventilation to allow water vapour to be transpired from the plants during the day.

The treatment of mildew is fairly straightforward these days and consists of regular spraying with a fungicide such as benomyl propiconazole, or spraying or dusting with sulphur, according to the manufacturers' instructions. I have found that a spray each month throughout the year with triforine with bupirimate, keeps begonias completely free from fungal diseases. Rex begonias, *B. masoniana*, tuberous species and hybrids, cane begonias and winter-flowering begonias are all susceptible to mildew, but fibrous-rooted and dwarf rhizomatous begonias never seem to be infected.

Botrytis is the other fungal growth that might take hold on begonias, evidenced by fluffy grey mould on or in a plant. It occurs under conditions of high humidity, as for mildew, when air circulation is restricted, particularly in a plant that has made a lot of thick growth in the centre and has become very congested. If it is found, the affected parts should be physically removed and the plant moved to an airier position and kept fairly dry, while treatment with a fungicide is carried out in the same

Opposite above: The leaf colouring of 'Cleopatra', a rhizomatous begonia, varies with light intensity
Below: *Begonia bowerae* has been the parent of numerous hybrids known as eyelash begonias

way as for mildew. Since this fungal growth needs high atmospheric humidity, it is not very often met with when begonias are grown as houseplants.

PESTS

Of recent years, vine weevils have become a major pest, not only to begonias, but to almost every type of plant, both indoors and outside. In pots, the larvae can soon destroy a plant by eating the root system and tuber, rhizome or stems, while the adult beetle will eat the leaves. Complete control is very difficult, since the adults can travel freely from the outside garden to the greenhouse or indoors. The incorporation of gamma-HCH in the potting compost does act somewhat as a deterrent to the pest. A better control is to treat the potting compost with the pathogenic nematode, *Heterorhabditis* sp. in late summer. Usually, the first indication that something is wrong is when the plant stops growing in its normally active season. Soon the leaves begin to get limp and droop as if lacking water. If the plant is examined, it may well fall out of its pot when it is picked up and it will be seen that the weevil larvae have eaten most of the plant material below soil level and have burrowed into the tuber, rhizome or stem. If this is the case, the remaining pieces of plant and the compost in the pot must be carefully searched for the white grub-like larvae, which should be removed and destroyed. What is left of the begonia can usually be repotted in fresh compost where it should re-root and grow again.

Tarsonemid mite is another pest that can affect begonias. The individuals are too small to be seen with the naked eye, but their presence is shown by the appearance of the new leaves, which emerge very distorted, often with a blackened edge, and soon acquire a dry, rusty look, then generally shrivel and drop off when only half-grown. Any leaves that do attain a reasonable size may have shrivelled brown patches on their edges and the undersides marked with dull, rusty brown streaks and patches. These leaves, too, soon become brittle and fall. Don't assume that mites are present, though, if some of the outer leaves on a plant become brown at the edges. This is to be expected on old leaves as they reach the end of their life. Control of this mite is difficult as the insecticides available to amateurs are ineffective. Plants showing symptoms should be destroyed.

Leaf and bud eelworms (*Aphelenchoides* spp.) are microscopic nematodes that live within the leaves causing yellowish-brown wedge shapes bounded by the larger leaf veins. Later the whole leaf discolours and drops off. As with tarsonemid mites, there

A group of mixed begonias: from left to right, a Superba hybrid,
B. angularis and 'Druryi' at the back; *B. glaziovii*, 'Lucerna Amazon' and
two Rex begonias in the middle; and 'Universe', 'Tiger Paws',
B. pustulata argentea and 'Chumash' in front

are no effective chemical controls available to amateur growers, so infested plants should be discarded.

Other well-known insects and pests such as whitefly, greenfly, scale insects and slugs do not seem to bother too much with begonias, but should such pests be seen on a plant, a wide range of insecticides is available, such as pirimicarb for greenfly and permethrin for whitefly. Mealybug may occasionally be found on Rex begonias. This can be controlled, by using malathion; spray damage can occur if used under hot sunny conditions.

The most common cause of leaf drop, particularly with cane-stemmed begonias, is overwatering, that is to say, keeping the compost constantly wet. Begonias have quite succulent stems and rhizomes and are able to accept dryness at the roots for a time owing to the moisture stored in the plant; provided this has not been so severe as to cause shrivelling of the leaves, water given to the roots will soon enable the plant to replace the water lost in the stems and to revert to its original appearance if it has drooped. The golden rule is to allow begonias to dry out at the roots between waterings.

Above: *Begonia haageana* (*scharffii*), a fibrous-rooted species which may reach over 5 ft (1.5 m) in height
Below: *Begonia albo-picta*, a miniature cane-stemmed species with arching stems

Above: The shrubby *Begonia angularis* should be grown in good light
Below: 'Chantilly Lace', a lovely dwarf rhizomatous hybrid of *B. bowerae*

Above: *Begonia manicata* originated in Mexico. This striking rhizomatous begonia is easy to grow

Opposite: *Begonia grandis evansiana*, a hardy tuberous species, makes a fine garden plant in southern England

Index

Page numbers in **bold** refer to illustrations